Behavior Modeling Training for Developing Supervisory Skills

Trainee Manual

Behavior Modeling Training for Developing Supervisory Skills

Trainee Manual

by

William M. Fox, PhD

IAP

Information Age Publishing, Inc.
Charlotte, North Carolina • www.infoagepub.com

ISBN: 978-1-60752-095-5

Printed in the United States of America

CONTENTS

Preface

This Trainee Manual is designed to be used in conjunction with an instructor-directed program based on material in *Behavior Modeling Training for Developing Supervisory Skills: Instructor Manual*, by the same author

Introduction

Too often, conventional means for dealing with subordinate-related problems fail to bring about desired changes in behavior or, worse still, make the subordinate defensive or resentful. Sound behavior-modeling training virtually assures success.

It provides easy-to-master stages and blow-by-blow guidelines. It will help you to create a fair, non-threatening work enviornment that will get results, while maintaining the self-esteem of your individual team members and enhancing the respect of all for your managerial skill.

Upon the successful completion of this training, you should:

- see the productivity of your unit go up,
- experience reduced stress in your job,
- improve relations with your subordinates, and
- become more promotable.

Behavior-modeling training is a form of skill-development training that is distinguished by the manner in which it integrates "knowledge about" and "experience with." Both of these elements are essential for effective skill training. To illustrate: think of what we must do to master some skill, such as dancing, driving a car, or making a presentation. We must go beyond merely reading about, hearing about, or observing the techniques involved—we must add guided practice, feedback, and adjusted practice.

Various sets of learning points—learning-point modules—have been developed for various training needs; such as, for Delegating Work, Handling a Complaining Employee, Handling Insubordination, Giving Recognition, Conducting a Performance-Review Interview, Mediating Between Conflicting Individuals, and so on. Examples of these, along with proecdures for developing new modules, are presented in the Instructor Manual. Your initial training will utilize two modules for Dealing With an Individual Performance Problem.

Basic Approach

There are four basic components of behavior modeling:

- learning points or instructions for mastering a skill,
- demonstration of the skill by a competent model,
- trainee practice with feedback, and
- follow-up, remedial action and reinforcement to encourage sustained mastery and transfer to non-training settings.

A number of other labels have been used for the basic behavior-modeling approach: applied learning, behavior modeling-interaction management (BMIM), behavioral rehearsal, behavioral replications technique, behavioral training, interactive modeling, interpersonal skills training, job instruction training (JIT), managerial skills training, social, skills training, structured learning therapy, and supervisory relationships training. Apparently, the term "behavior modeling" did not appear before the 1970s.

Demonstrated Effectiveness

The results from numerous research studies indicate that behavior modeling—when properly used—provides the most effective approach we have today for skill-development training.[1]

Assignment to a Group

Prior to the practice session, you will be assigned to groups of four or three. Small training groups are preferable because:

- You will not have to go "on stage" and confront a large audience when you undertake the more demanding supervisory role.
- You will benefit from playing the role of a subordinate and from observing your fellow group members enact their roles, as you prepare to provide them with feedback in your role as an observer.

Assignment of a Roleset

The instructor will give you a W, X, Y, or Z Roleset if you are in a four-person group, or a T, U, or V Roleset if you are in a three-person group. The roles you will receive are particularly suited to your first practice session, because:

- They are relatively brief and of limited complexity. This will help you to get accustomed to using the learning points in a roleplay setting.
- They will provide a common postpractice experience to discuss and evaluate, since all groups will have used the same roleplays.

Note: To enhance the realism of your roleplaying, and thereby gain more benefit from the practice experience, *do not look at each other's Rolesets until after the practice session.*

PREPARING FOR YOUR FIRST PRACTICE SESSION

- Read the exercise instructions presented on the first page of your Roleset
- Study the role of the supervisor and the role of the subordinate you will play
- Read the discussion below of the two modules for dealing with an individual performance problem, *Nonjudgmental Information Gathering* and *Remedial Action* and think about how you will use these learning points in your interview with a subordinate.
- Study the instructions on both pages of the *Observer Form.*

Remember to take your Roleset and this Manual to the first practice session.

Discussion of the Nonjudgmental Information Gathering Learning Points

Note: This module should be used before the *Remedial Action* module, and only one problem should be dealt with at a time, so that the interviewer can remain better focused and have a better chance of achieving constructive closure.

- **Explain, specifically, what you are concerned about and why you feel it is a problem, presenting any objective evidence you have, while withholding judgment of the person.**

Too often, we go off "half-cocked" with what turns out to be incomplete information and/or misperceptions—we assume that we *know* which problems exist and just what they are. The best protection against this danger is to present our perceptions as objectively as possible with the idea of encouraging the other person to give as full a response as he or she wishes to.

The other person will not feel as free to respond, or to do so in as constructive a manner, if he or she perceives us to be making an unwarranted accusation, or to be showing in our tone or manner that we have already determined the extent of "guilt" before a fair hearing.

True, you can unfairly chew someone out, and then apologize later when you discover that you were wrong, but why do needless damage, and jeopardize a relationship, when you don't have to?

- **Listen nonjudgmentally—to give person full opportunity to explain events and/or feelings—and encourage responding with comments, such as: "I see," "Can you tell me more about such and such?" and "What happened then?"**

It is not enough to *start off* objectively and nonjudgmentally, you must *stay this way* until the person has given as full a response as he or she wishes to. Premature arguments, contradictions, and judgments can "turn off" constructive responding in a hurry.

Being nonjudgmental does not signify agreement with what is being said. If the person asks "Don't you agree?" You can respond: "My only purpose right now is to try to fully understand your position and feelings about this."

- **When there is much input, "mirror back" what you have heard to check your understanding—for example: "As I understand it, you did this, because..." or, "You feel that you have been unfairly accused, because ..."**

Actually, the term "much input" should be expanded to say: "much, or complex, or ambiguous input."

This learning point must be used with discretion. It would be inappropriate to mirror back every statement that a person makes. On the other hand, you should use mirroring if you are in doubt about what was said or there is a chance that you missed important details.

In addition, you should use mirroring when a person seems confused or inconsistent. Hearing a difficult or confused thought played back from another source can have a beneficial effect on one's thinking.

Appropriate mirroring also provides reassurance to a person that you really do understand his or her position and feelings.

- **When needed, set a specific date for a follow-up meeting, to permit you to collect information from**

other sources and/or to prepare for the next module, *Remedial Action*.

At times, you can go right into the remedial-action phase. However, there are other times when it would be prudent to confirm the information provided by just one person, or to gather other viewpoints which might alter your perception of the situation. When this is the case, time permitting, you should check with other sources and set a specific date for a follow-up meeting.

But *for this exercise*, you must try to resolve the situation with the information at hand, *not* delay action for further investigation as is often appropriate in real-life implementation.

Discussion of the Remedial Action Learning Points

Note: This module should be preceded by the *Non-judgmental Information Gathering* module, and only one problem should be dealt with at a time, so that the interviewer can remain better focused and have a better chance of achieving constructive closure.

- **State any solution requirements person may not be aware of.**

It can be frustrating and time wasting to develop a "solution" that cannot be used due to technical, policy, or other constraints.

Furthermore, there are times when an enumeration of *all* requirements will turn up conflicts or competing priorities that will have to be resolved before the present problem can be dealt with effectively.

If you have any doubt about the possession of this knowledge on the part of the person you are dealing with (or yourself), clearly determine and spell out the requirements that a solution must satisfy.

- **If a simple solution is not apparent, solicit and record person's ideas for solving the problem (on a blackboard or flipchart where both of you can see them)—giving no evaluation on your part at this time.**

If a good solution to a relatively simple problem is rather obvious, there is no need to put it on display. When this is not the case, you can best encourage the other person to share his or her thinking—and be creative—by having him or her contribute *first,* and by *not* evaluating this input at this point.

- **Add your ideas—without evaluating them—then add any additional ones that occur to either of you.**

Your creativity will also benefit from adherence to this deferred evaluation rule.

Seeing the items on display can stimulate both of you to develop additional ideas to add. They need not be completely original, for originality is less important than producing a good, mutually acceptable solution. It is productive to build on each other's thinking.

- **Discuss and evaluate the ideas in terms of "pros" and "cons" associated with each (including the option of "no action").**

An acceptable solution must satisfy all constraints. In addition, it must be evaluated in terms of any weights or priorities that have been established.

If two solutions are equally acceptable to you, go with the one that is most acceptable to the other person.

Often, we fail to deal with "no action" as an alternative solution that needs to be evaluated. This is a mistake. Whatever the reason for assuming a "no action" course, it will have effects that will be just as real as those for an "action" course.

- **Seek agreement on a solution and spell out the specific steps to be taken by either, or both, of you. If you cannot agree, and you have supervisory authority over the person, specify the action you will require, your reasons for requiring it, and when you expect it to occur *(then skip the next step).***

Unless the problem was merely a misunderstanding, it will not be solved until words are converted into action.

Research findings show that "do your best" action goals are not as motivating as ones that are specific, challenging, understood, and accepted.

- **Mirror back what other is committed to (as a check on understanding; for example, saying: "As I understand it, you will do such and such"—accurately playing back what you have heard).**

- **Agree on a specific, follow-up meeting, or observation time and date, for reviewing progress or results.**

The setting of a follow-up time and date for observation (checking on results), or a meeting, assures a basis for determining whether or not the problem is really solved.

It also provides a definite basis for establishing accountability for remedial action, and it is a form of goal setting that will better motivate you and the other person to follow through on your commitments.

In addition, a definite meeting time and date assures that the person will have access to you—it will be on your calendar—and she or he will not have to worry about when and if to intrude on your busy schedule. Saying, "Check with me in 2 weeks," is far more likely to lead to delay or total forgetting.

An exception to this, of course, is when the person works in the same office with you every day. Then, you may need only a "reminder" note on your calendar to deal with the matter.

- **Praise the person as soon as possible after successful implementation occurs (or for completion of a first step in a series of steps).**

Research in behavior management shows that the timing of positive reinforcement has an important effect on its motivational value: the sooner after the desired behavior or event, the better.

In addition, research findings show that *specificity* and *location* are important:

- you should be quite specific about what you are giving praise for;
- the first and primary place for giving the praise should be the person's work station rather than the water cooler, the lunch counter, or some other place.

True, the above guidelines for giving praise may seem trivial or illogical, but there is abundant evidence that we are not as rational as we like to believe: Giving praise at the water cooler, will tend to subconsciously, reinforce going to the water cooler!

Background Overview

Historical records indicate that Behavior Modeling was used by instructors in specialized Roman schools for training gladiators. This was illustrated in the film *Spartacus* in which one of the film stars, Kirk Douglas, attended such a school.

We also know that instructors in other fields—sports, medicine, the theater, and various trades—discovered the merits of behavior modeling a long time ago, because the approach is so intuitively appealing and effective.

Apparently, the first detailed discussion of behavior-modeling concepts was written by C. H. Woodward in 1887 for guiding the development of manual skills.[2] Then, in 1918, Charles Allen, director of training for the U.S. Emergency Fleet Corporation in World War I, used behavior modeling to train more than 1,000 shipyard instructors.[3]

Building upon this work, Glen Gardiner and M. J. Kane developed the highly successful Job Instruction Training (JIT) component of the Training Within Industry (TWI) program of, World War II. From August 1940 to September 1945, four national directors trained 22 regional directors. They, in turn, trained 200 TWI Institute conductors. Eventually, 23,000 trainers effectively trained some 1.75 million supervisors in 16,500 plants![4]

There is a 1942 report of Behavior Modeling being used for therapeutic purposes,[5] and several reports of its usage for supervisory skills training during the mid-1970s.[6]

Today, we know that consistent results with it require adequate attention to all four components, and we have the benefit of research findings that indicate how to improve the effectiveness of each component. In addition, we have the benefit of well-developed and valid supporting theory by Albert Bandura (see his 1986 work, *Social Foundations of Thought and Action: A Social Cognitive Theory*).

NOTES

1. See H. J. Burke and R. R. Day, "A Cumulative Study of the Effectiveness of Management Training," *Journal of Applied Psychology,* 1986, *71,* 232-245. Also, Paul Taylor's meta-analysis of 97 studies which shows that behavior modeling has been effective in a variety of international settings ("The Transferability of Behavior Modeling Training Across Organizations and Cultures," paper presented at the July, 1994 International HRM Conference in Queensland, Australia). In addition, the author found strong, significant effects for four-component, behavior modeling training in his review of 43 single-skill-area training studies and 13 multiple-module, supervisory skills training studies. Only five studies were associated with weak or missing effects; however, results were often equivocal when one of more of the components had been omitted.

2. C. M. Woodward, *The Manual Training School.* Boston: D. C. Heath and Company, 1887.

3. C. R. Allen, *The Instructor, The Man and The Job.* Philadelphia: J. P. Lippincott, 1919.

4. U.S. Government Printing Office, *The Training Within Industry Report, 1940-1945,* September 1945, especially chapter 7.

5. G. E. Chittenden, "An Experimental Study in Measuring and Modifying Assertive Behavior in Young Children," *Monographs of the Society for Research in Child Development,* 1942, 7(1).

6. A. E. Kraut, "Developing Managerial Skill Via Modeling Techniques: Some Positive Research Findings—A Symposium," *Personnel Psychology,* 1976, *29,* 325-328; A. P. Goldstein and H. Sorcher, *Changing Supervisory Behavior.* New York: Pergamon Press, 1974.

Appendix of Detachable Forms

Learning Points Worksheet

Learning Points	*Make checkmark (below) each time the Learning Point is used*
Explain, specifically, what you are concerned about and why you think it is a problem, presenting any objective evidence you have, while withholding judgment of the person	
Listen nonjudgmentally—to give person full opportunity to explain events and/or feelings—and encourage responding with comments, such as, "I see," "Can you tell me more about such and such," and "What happened then?"	
When there is much input, "mirror back" what you have heard to check your understanding—for example: "As I understand it, you did this because ..." or, "You feel that you have been unfairly accused because ..."	
When needed, set a specific date for a follow-up meeting, to permit you to collect information from other sources and/or to prepare for the next module, *Remedial Action*	(not applicable in practice session)

Note: For this exercise, the person playing supervisor must try to resolve the situation with the information at hand, not delay action for further investigation, as is often appropriate in real-life implementation.

(Begin *Remedial Action* learning points)

State any solution requirements person may not be aware of	
If a simple solution is not apparent, solicit and record person's ideas for solving problem (on a blackboard or flipchart where both of you can see them)—giving no evaluation on your part at this time	
Add your ideas—without evaluating them—then add any additional ones that occur to either of you	
Discuss and evaluate the ideas in terms of "pros" and "cons" associated with each (including the option of "no action")	
Seek agreement on a solution and spell out specific steps to be taken by either or both of you. If you cannot agree and you have supervisory authority over the person, specify the action you will require, your reasons for requiring it, and when you expect it to occur	
When there is much input, "mirror back" what other is committed to as a check on understanding; for example, saying "As I understand it, you will do such and such"	
Agree on a specific follow-up meeting or observation time and date for reviewing progress or results	
Praise person as soon as possible after successful implementation occurs (or for completion of a first step in a series of steps)	(not applicable in practice session)

Learning Points Worksheet

Learning Points	*Make checkmark (below) each time the Learning Point is used*
Explain, specifically, what you are concerned about and why you think it is a problem, presenting any objective evidence you have, while withholding judgment of the person	
Listen nonjudgmentally—to give person full opportunity to explain events and/or feelings—and encourage responding with comments, such as, "I see," "Can you tell me more about such and such," and "What happened then?"	
When there is much input, "mirror back" what you have heard to check your understanding—for example: "As I understand it, you did this because ..." or, "You feel that you have been unfairly accused because ..."	
When needed, set a specific date for a follow-up meeting, to permit you to collect information from other sources and/or to prepare for the next module, *Remedial Action*	(not applicable in practice session)

Note: For this exercise, the person playing supervisor must try to resolve the situation with the information at hand, not delay action for further investigation, as is often appropriate in real-life implementation.

(Begin *Remedial Action* learning points)

State any solution requirements person may not be aware of	
If a simple solution is not apparent, solicit and record person's ideas for solving problem (on a blackboard or flipchart where both of you can see them)—giving no evaluation on your part at this time	
Add your ideas—without evaluating them—then add any additional ones that occur to either of you	
Discuss and evaluate the ideas in terms of "pros" and "cons" associated with each (including the option of "no action")	
Seek agreement on a solution and spell out specific steps to be taken by either or both of you. If you cannot agree and you have supervisory authority over the person, specify the action you will require, your reasons for requiring it, and when you expect it to occur	
When there is much input, "mirror back" what other is committed to as a check on understanding; for example, saying "As I understand it, you will do such and such"	
Agree on a specific follow-up meeting or observation time and date for reviewing progress or results	
Praise person as soon as possible after successful implementation occurs (or for completion of a first step in a series of steps)	(not applicable in practice session)

Learning Points Worksheet

Learning Points	*Make checkmark (below) each time the Learning Point is used*
Explain, specifically, what you are concerned about and why you think it is a problem, presenting any objective evidence you have, while withholding judgment of the person	
Listen nonjudgmentally—to give person full opportunity to explain events and/or feelings—and encourage responding with comments, such as, "I see," "Can you tell me more about such and such," and "What happened then?"	
When there is much input, "mirror back" what you have heard to check your understanding—for example: "As I understand it, you did this because …" or, "You feel that you have been unfairly accused because …"	
When needed, set a specific date for a follow-up meeting, to permit you to collect information from other sources and/or to prepare for the next module, *Remedial Action*	(not applicable in practice session)

Note: For this exercise, the person playing supervisor must try to resolve the situation with the information at hand, not delay action for further investigation, as is often appropriate in real-life implementation.

(Begin *Remedial Action* learning points)

State any solution requirements person may not be aware of	
If a simple solution is not apparent, solicit and record person's ideas for solving problem (on a blackboard or flipchart where both of you can see them)—giving no evaluation on your part at this time	
Add your ideas—without evaluating them—then add any additional ones that occur to either of you	
Discuss and evaluate the ideas in terms of "pros" and "cons" associated with each (including the option of "no action")	
Seek agreement on a solution and spell out specific steps to be taken by either or both of you. If you cannot agree and you have supervisory authority over the person, specify the action you will require, your reasons for requiring it, and when you expect it to occur	
When there is much input, "mirror back" what other is committed to as a check on understanding; for example, saying "As I understand it, you will do such and such"	
Agree on a specific follow-up meeting or observation time and date for reviewing progress or results	
Praise person as soon as possible after successful implementation occurs (or for completion of a first step in a series of steps)	(not applicable in practice session)

Learning Points Worksheet

Learning Points	*Make checkmark (below) each time the Learning Point is used*
Explain, specifically, what you are concerned about and why you think it is a problem, presenting any objective evidence you have, while withholding judgment of the person	
Listen nonjudgmentally—to give person full opportunity to explain events and/or feelings—and encourage responding with comments, such as, "I see," "Can you tell me more about such and such," and "What happened then?"	
When there is much input, "mirror back" what you have heard to check your understanding—for example: "As I understand it, you did this because ..." or, "You feel that you have been unfairly accused because ..."	
When needed, set a specific date for a follow-up meeting, to permit you to collect information from other sources and/or to prepare for the next module, *Remedial Action*	(not applicable in practice session)

Note: For this exercise, the person playing supervisor must try to resolve the situation with the information at hand, not delay action for further investigation, as is often appropriate in real-life implementation.

(Begin *Remedial Action* learning points)

State any solution requirements person may not be aware of	
If a simple solution is not apparent, solicit and record person's ideas for solving problem (on a blackboard or flipchart where both of you can see them)—giving no evaluation on your part at this time	
Add your ideas—without evaluating them—then add any additional ones that occur to either of you	
Discuss and evaluate the ideas in terms of "pros" and "cons" associated with each (including the option of "no action")	
Seek agreement on a solution and spell out specific steps to be taken by either or both of you. If you cannot agree and you have supervisory authority over the person, specify the action you will require, your reasons for requiring it, and when you expect it to occur	
When there is much input, "mirror back" what other is committed to as a check on understanding; for example, saying "As I understand it, you will do such and such"	
Agree on a specific follow-up meeting or observation time and date for reviewing progress or results	
Praise person as soon as possible after successful implementation occurs (or for completion of a first step in a series of steps)	(not applicable in practice session)

Learning Points Worksheet

Learning Points	***Make checkmark (below) each time the Learning Point is used***
Explain, specifically, what you are concerned about and why you think it is a problem, presenting any objective evidence you have, while withholding judgment of the person	
Listen nonjudgmentally—to give person full opportunity to explain events and/or feelings—and encourage responding with comments, such as, "I see," "Can you tell me more about such and such," and "What happened then?"	
When there is much input, "mirror back" what you have heard to check your understanding—for example: "As I understand it, you did this because ..." or, "You feel that you have been unfairly accused because ..."	
When needed, set a specific date for a follow-up meeting, to permit you to collect information from other sources and/or to prepare for the next module, *Remedial Action*	(not applicable in practice session)

Note: For this exercise, the person playing supervisor must try to resolve the situation with the information at hand, not delay action for further investigation, as is often appropriate in real-life implementation.

(Begin *Remedial Action* learning points)

State any solution requirements person may not be aware of	
If a simple solution is not apparent, solicit and record person's ideas for solving problem (on a blackboard or flipchart where both of you can see them)—giving no evaluation on your part at this time	
Add your ideas—without evaluating them—then add any additional ones that occur to either of you	
Discuss and evaluate the ideas in terms of "pros" and "cons" associated with each (including the option of "no action")	
Seek agreement on a solution and spell out specific steps to be taken by either or both of you. If you cannot agree and you have supervisory authority over the person, specify the action you will require, your reasons for requiring it, and when you expect it to occur	
When there is much input, "mirror back" what other is committed to as a check on understanding; for example, saying "As I understand it, you will do such and such"	
Agree on a specific follow-up meeting or observation time and date for reviewing progress or results	
Praise person as soon as possible after successful implementation occurs (or for completion of a first step in a series of steps)	(not applicable in practice session)

Learning Points Refresher Sheet

(Use as a reminder for rolelplays and on the job)

Nonjudgmental Information Gathering (Precedes *Remedial Action*)	*Remedial Action*
Explain specifically, what you are concerned about, and why you think it is a problem. Listen nonjudgmentally for full explanation. When there is much input, "mirror" what you have heard, giving no evaluation. When further information gathering is needed, set a specific date for a follow-up meeting.	• State any solution requirements person may not be aware of. • If simple solution is not apparent, solicit and record person's ideas for solving the problem, giving no evaluation. • Add your ideas without evaluating them, then additional ones that occur to either of you. • Discuss the pros and cons of the ideas. • Seek agreement on a solution that specifies steps to be taken (if no agreement can be reached, indicate what you will require, giving reasons, and set a deadline for compliance.) • "Mirror back" what other is committed to (as a check on understanding). • Agree on a specific follow-up meeting or observation time and date (to review progress or results). • Immediately praise person for any progress toward a goal.

Observer Form

When you act as an *Observer*:

- Remind the person playing Supervisor to *mentally rehearse* (briefly) how s/he will implement the learning points before s/he starts the roleplay.
- As the roleplay takes place, *use the form below* to indicate by each of the learning points whether or not s/he implemented it. (Note: "Did not apply is an option on all but the first two scales).
- Check how well the roleplayers comply with the assumptions of their roles as indicated by the descriptions in your *Roleset*. (Each player received one of these descriptions.)
- Keep time, to see that the roleplay does not take more than 8 minutes, so that subsequent-round roleplayers will not be shortchanged.

See additional instructions after the Learning Points

	Did Not Apply	*Yes*	*No*	*Somewhat*
Initially, s/he explained the performance concern objectively, without prematurely judging interviewee or being critical.	____	____	____	____
S/he gave interviewee ample opportunity to explain what happened and/or express feelings.	____	____	____	____
When appropriate, s/he summarized or "played back" what interviewee had said.	____	____	____	____
S/he set a specific date for a follow-up meeting to permit further data collection or preparation for solving the problem.	____	____	____	____
S/he stated solution requirements that interviewee was not aware of.	____	____	____	____
In a noncritical and friendly way, s/he solicited and recorded interviewee's ideas first for solving the problem.	____	____	____	____
S/he presented his/her ideas for solving the problem (after the interviewee).	____	____	____	____
Together, they evaluated the "pros" and "cons" of each idea (this could include the choice of "no action").	____	____	____	____
They agreed on a solution that made clear any steps to be taken by each.	____	____	____	____
S/he summarized what interviewee was committed to do (to avoid any misunderstanding).	____	____	____	____
They agreed on a specific time and date for a follow-up meeting (or assessment of results).	____	____	____	____
At the end of the interview, s/he felt there was a problem. Though they had ample discussion, they could not agree on a solution. Then s/he explained explicitly what interviewee would have to do.	____	____	____	____

When the Roleplay ends: Eight minutes total is allocated for the activities below (whether performed by one or two observers). ***IMPORTANT:*** Perform activities in the order given.

1. Ask the person playing the Subordinate:

    - What in the interview seemed most helpful to you?
    - Was there anything negative?
    - What would you do as a result of the interview?

2. Indicate to the person playing Supervisor:

    - Any applicable learning points that were overlooked, or were implemented at the wrong time.
    - Extent to which s/he came across as being sincere.
    - Praise for learning points that were well executed (indicating the specific ones).

3. Solicit reactions from the person playing Supervisor.

Note: If the full 16 minutes for the round have not been used by the end of the Supervisor's comments, s/he may want to use the remaining time to repeat a specific part of the interview that was deficient.

Observer Form

When you act as an *Observer*:

- Remind the person playing Supervisor to *mentally rehearse* (briefly) how s/he will implement the learning points before s/he starts the roleplay.
- As the roleplay takes place, *use the form below* to indicate by each of the learning points whether or not s/he implemented it. (Note: "Did not apply is an option on all but the first two scales).
- Check how well the roleplayers comply with the assumptions of their roles as indicated by the descriptions in your *Roleset*. (Each player received one of these descriptions.)
- Keep time, to see that the roleplay does not take more than 8 minutes, so that subsequent-round roleplayers will not be shortchanged.

See additional instructions after the Learning Points

	Did Not Apply	*Yes*	*No*	*Somewhat*
Initially, s/he explained the performance concern objectively, without prematurely judging interviewee or being critical.	____	____	____	____
S/he gave interviewee ample opportunity to explain what happened and/or express feelings.	____	____	____	____
When appropriate, s/he summarized or "played back" what interviewee had said.	____	____	____	____
S/he set a specific date for a follow-up meeting to permit further data collection or preparation for solving the problem.	____	____	____	____
S/he stated solution requirements that interviewee was not aware of.	____	____	____	____
In a noncritical and friendly way, s/he solicited and recorded interviewee's ideas first for solving the problem.	____	____	____	____
S/he presented his/her ideas for solving the problem (after the interviewee).	____	____	____	____
Together, they evaluated the "pros" and "cons" of each idea (this could include the choice of "no action").	____	____	____	____
They agreed on a solution that made clear any steps to be taken by each.	____	____	____	____
S/he summarized what interviewee was committed to do (to avoid any misunderstanding).	____	____	____	____
They agreed on a specific time and date for a follow-up meeting (or assessment of results).	____	____	____	____
At the end of the interview, s/he felt there was a problem. Though they had ample discussion, they could not agree on a solution. Then s/he explained explicitly what interviewee would have to do.	____	____	____	____

When the Roleplay ends: Eight minutes total is allocated for the activities below (whether performed by one or two observers). ***IMPORTANT***: Perform activities in the order given.

1. Ask the person playing the Subordinate:

    - What in the interview seemed most helpful to you?
    - Was there anything negative?
    - What would you do as a result of the interview?

2. Indicate to the person playing Supervisor:

    - Any applicable learning points that were overlooked, or were implemented at the wrong time.
    - Extent to which s/he came across as being sincere.
    - Praise for learning points that were well executed (indicating the specific ones).

3. Solicit reactions from the person playing Supervisor.

Note: If the full 16 minutes for the round have not been used by the end of the Supervisor's comments, s/he may want to use the remaining time to repeat a specific part of the interview that was deficient.

Observer Form

When you act as an *Observer*:

- Remind the person playing Supervisor to *mentally rehearse* (briefly) how s/he will implement the learning points before s/he starts the roleplay.
- As the roleplay takes place, *use the form below* to indicate by each of the learning points whether or not s/he implemented it. (Note: "Did not apply is an option on all but the first two scales).
- Check how well the roleplayers comply with the assumptions of their roles as indicated by the descriptions in your *Roleset*. (Each player received one of these descriptions.)
- Keep time, to see that the roleplay does not take more than 8 minutes, so that subsequent-round roleplayers will not be shortchanged.

See additional instructions after the Learning Points

	Did Not Apply	*Yes*	*No*	*Somewhat*
Initially, s/he explained the performance concern objectively, without prematurely judging interviewee or being critical.	____	____	____	____
S/he gave interviewee ample opportunity to explain what happened and/or express feelings.	____	____	____	____
When appropriate, s/he summarized or "played back" what interviewee had said.	____	____	____	____
S/he set a specific date for a follow-up meeting to permit further data collection or preparation for solving the problem.	____	____	____	____
S/he stated solution requirements that interviewee was not aware of.	____	____	____	____
In a noncritical and friendly way, s/he solicited and recorded interviewee's ideas first for solving the problem.	____	____	____	____
S/he presented his/her ideas for solving the problem (after the interviewee).	____	____	____	____
Together, they evaluated the "pros" and "cons" of each idea (this could include the choice of "no action").	____	____	____	____
They agreed on a solution that made clear any steps to be taken by each.	____	____	____	____
S/he summarized what interviewee was committed to do (to avoid any misunderstanding).	____	____	____	____
They agreed on a specific time and date for a follow-up meeting (or assessment of results).	____	____	____	____
At the end of the interview, s/he felt there was a problem. Though they had ample discussion, they could not agree on a solution. Then s/he explained explicitly what interviewee would have to do.	____	____	____	____

When the Roleplay ends: Eight minutes total is allocated for the activities below (whether performed by one or two observers). ***IMPORTANT:*** Perform activities in the order given.

1. Ask the person playing the Subordinate:

    - What in the interview seemed most helpful to you?
    - Was there anything negative?
    - What would you do as a result of the interview?

2. Indicate to the person playing Supervisor:

    - Any applicable learning points that were overlooked, or were implemented at the wrong time.
    - Extent to which s/he came across as being sincere.
    - Praise for learning points that were well executed (indicating the specific ones).

3. Solicit reactions from the person playing Supervisor.

Note: If the full 16 minutes for the round have not been used by the end of the Supervisor's comments, s/he may want to use the remaining time to repeat a specific part of the interview that was deficient.

Observer Form

When you act as an *Observer*:

- Remind the person playing Supervisor to *mentally rehearse* (briefly) how s/he will implement the learning points before s/he starts the roleplay.
- As the roleplay takes place, *use the form below* to indicate by each of the learning points whether or not s/he implemented it. (Note: "Did not apply is an option on all but the first two scales).
- Check how well the roleplayers comply with the assumptions of their roles as indicated by the descriptions in your *Roleset*. (Each player received one of these descriptions.)
- Keep time, to see that the roleplay does not take more than 8 minutes, so that subsequent-round roleplayers will not be shortchanged.

See additional instructions after the Learning Points

	Did Not Apply	*Yes*	*No*	*Somewhat*
Initially, s/he explained the performance concern objectively, without prematurely judging interviewee or being critical.	____	____	____	____
S/he gave interviewee ample opportunity to explain what happened and/or express feelings.	____	____	____	____
When appropriate, s/he summarized or "played back" what interviewee had said.	____	____	____	____
S/he set a specific date for a follow-up meeting to permit further data collection or preparation for solving the problem.	____	____	____	____
S/he stated solution requirements that interviewee was not aware of.	____	____	____	____
In a noncritical and friendly way, s/he solicited and recorded interviewee's ideas first for solving the problem.	____	____	____	____
S/he presented his/her ideas for solving the problem (after the interviewee).	____	____	____	____
Together, they evaluated the "pros" and "cons" of each idea (this could include the choice of "no action").	____	____	____	____
They agreed on a solution that made clear any steps to be taken by each.	____	____	____	____
S/he summarized what interviewee was committed to do (to avoid any misunderstanding).	____	____	____	____
They agreed on a specific time and date for a follow-up meeting (or assessment of results).	____	____	____	____
At the end of the interview, s/he felt there was a problem. Though they had ample discussion, they could not agree on a solution. Then s/he explained explicitly what interviewee would have to do.	____	____	____	____

When the Roleplay ends: Eight minutes total is allocated for the activities below (whether performed by one or two observers). ***IMPORTANT***: Perform activities in the order given.

1. Ask the person playing the Subordinate:

    - What in the interview seemed most helpful to you?
    - Was there anything negative?
    - What would you do as a result of the interview?

2. Indicate to the person playing Supervisor:

    - Any applicable learning points that were overlooked, or were implemented at the wrong time.
    - Extent to which s/he came across as being sincere.
    - Praise for learning points that were well executed (indicating the specific ones).

3. Solicit reactions from the person playing Supervisor.

Note: If the full 16 minutes for the round have not been used by the end of the Supervisor's comments, s/he may want to use the remaining time to repeat a specific part of the interview that was deficient.

Observer Form

When you act as an *Observer*:

- Remind the person playing Supervisor to *mentally rehearse* (briefly) how s/he will implement the learning points before s/he starts the roleplay.
- As the roleplay takes place, *use the form below* to indicate by each of the learning points whether or not s/he implemented it. (Note: "Did not apply is an option on all but the first two scales).
- Check how well the roleplayers comply with the assumptions of their roles as indicated by the descriptions in your *Roleset*. (Each player received one of these descriptions.)
- Keep time, to see that the roleplay does not take more than 8 minutes, so that subsequent-round roleplayers will not be shortchanged.

See additional instructions after the Learning Points

	Did Not Apply	*Yes*	*No*	*Somewhat*
Initially, s/he explained the performance concern objectively, without prematurely judging interviewee or being critical.	____	____	____	____
S/he gave interviewee ample opportunity to explain what happened and/or express feelings.	____	____	____	____
When appropriate, s/he summarized or "played back" what interviewee had said.	____	____	____	____
S/he set a specific date for a follow-up meeting to permit further data collection or preparation for solving the problem.	____	____	____	____
S/he stated solution requirements that interviewee was not aware of.	____	____	____	____
In a noncritical and friendly way, s/he solicited and recorded interviewee's ideas first for solving the problem.	____	____	____	____
S/he presented his/her ideas for solving the problem (after the interviewee).	____	____	____	____
Together, they evaluated the "pros" and "cons" of each idea (this could include the choice of "no action").	____	____	____	____
They agreed on a solution that made clear any steps to be taken by each.	____	____	____	____
S/he summarized what interviewee was committed to do (to avoid any misunderstanding).	____	____	____	____
They agreed on a specific time and date for a follow-up meeting (or assessment of results).	____	____	____	____
At the end of the interview, s/he felt there was a problem. Though they had ample discussion, they could not agree on a solution. Then s/he explained explicitly what interviewee would have to do.	____	____	____	____

When the Roleplay ends: Eight minutes total is allocated for the activities below (whether performed by one or two observers). ***IMPORTANT:*** Perform activities in the order given.

1. Ask the person playing the Subordinate:

    - What in the interview seemed most helpful to you?
    - Was there anything negative?
    - What would you do as a result of the interview?

2. Indicate to the person playing Supervisor:

    - Any applicable learning points that were overlooked, or were implemented at the wrong time.
    - Extent to which s/he came across as being sincere.
    - Praise for learning points that were well executed (indicating the specific ones).

3. Solicit reactions from the person playing Supervisor.

Note: If the full 16 minutes for the round have not been used by the end of the Supervisor's comments, s/he may want to use the remaining time to repeat a specific part of the interview that was deficient.

Observer Form

When you act as an *Observer*:

- Remind the person playing Supervisor to *mentally rehearse* (briefly) how s/he will implement the learning points before s/he starts the roleplay.
- As the roleplay takes place, *use the form below* to indicate by each of the learning points whether or not s/he implemented it. (Note: "Did not apply is an option on all but the first two scales).
- Check how well the roleplayers comply with the assumptions of their roles as indicated by the descriptions in your *Roleset*. (Each player received one of these descriptions.)
- Keep time, to see that the roleplay does not take more than 8 minutes, so that subsequent-round roleplayers will not be shortchanged.

See additional instructions after the Learning Points

	Did Not Apply	*Yes*	*No*	*Somewhat*
Initially, s/he explained the performance concern objectively, without prematurely judging interviewee or being critical.	____	____	____	____
S/he gave interviewee ample opportunity to explain what happened and/or express feelings.	____	____	____	____
When appropriate, s/he summarized or "played back" what interviewee had said.	____	____	____	____
S/he set a specific date for a follow-up meeting to permit further data collection or preparation for solving the problem.	____	____	____	____
S/he stated solution requirements that interviewee was not aware of.	____	____	____	____
In a noncritical and friendly way, s/he solicited and recorded interviewee's ideas first for solving the problem.	____	____	____	____
S/he presented his/her ideas for solving the problem (after the interviewee).	____	____	____	____
Together, they evaluated the "pros" and "cons" of each idea (this could include the choice of "no action").	____	____	____	____
They agreed on a solution that made clear any steps to be taken by each.	____	____	____	____
S/he summarized what interviewee was committed to do (to avoid any misunderstanding).	____	____	____	____
They agreed on a specific time and date for a follow-up meeting (or assessment of results).	____	____	____	____
At the end of the interview, s/he felt there was a problem. Though they had ample discussion, they could not agree on a solution. Then s/he explained explicitly what interviewee would have to do.	____	____	____	____

When the Roleplay ends: Eight minutes total is allocated for the activities below (whether performed by one or two observers). ***IMPORTANT***: Perform activities in the order given.

1. Ask the person playing the Subordinate:
   - What in the interview seemed most helpful to you?
   - Was there anything negative?
   - What would you do as a result of the interview?
2. Indicate to the person playing Supervisor:
   - Any applicable learning points that were overlooked, or were implemented at the wrong time.
   - Extent to which s/he came across as being sincere.
   - Praise for learning points that were well executed (indicating the specific ones).
3. Solicit reactions from the person playing Supervisor.

Note: If the full 16 minutes for the round have not been used by the end of the Supervisor's comments, s/he may want to use the remaining time to repeat a specific part of the interview that was deficient.

End-of-Practice-Session Questionnaire

How do you rate the live demonstration or videotape you saw today? (Please check one)

Unacceptable	Poor	Average	Above Average	Excellent

Do you have any suggestions for improving it for future use?

To what extent did you feel that you were in a realistic situation as you completed your roleplay as Supervisor?

To No Extent	Little Extent	Great Extent	Completely

Have you any suggestions for improving the roleplays or for improving the procedure for using them?

What is your reaction to behavior modeling as a training approach?

Other comments or suggestions

End-of-Practice-Session Questionnaire

How do you rate the live demonstration or videotape you saw today? (Please check one)

Unacceptable	Poor	Average	Above Average	Excellent
___	___	___	___	___

Do you have any suggestions for improving it for future use?

____

____

____

____

To what extent did you feel that you were in a realistic situation as you completed your roleplay as Supervisor?

To No Extent	Little Extent	Great Extent	Completely
___	___	___	___

Have you any suggestions for improving the roleplays or for improving the procedure for using them?

____

____

____

____

What is your reaction to behavior modeling as a training approach?

____

____

____

____

Other comments or suggestions ______________________________

____

____

____

____

____

____

End-of-Practice-Session Questionnaire

How do you rate the live demonstration or videotape you saw today? (Please check one)

Unacceptable	Poor	Average	Above Average	Excellent

Do you have any suggestions for improving it for future use?

To what extent did you feel that you were in a realistic situation as you completed your roleplay as Supervisor?

To No Extent	Little Extent	Great Extent	Completely

Have you any suggestions for improving the roleplays or for improving the procedure for using them?

What is your reaction to behavior modeling as a training approach?

Other comments or suggestions

End-of-Practice-Session Questionnaire

How do you rate the live demonstration or videotape you saw today? (Please check one)

Unacceptable	Poor	Average	Above Average	Excellent

Do you have any suggestions for improving it for future use?

To what extent did you feel that you were in a realistic situation as you completed your roleplay as Supervisor?

To No Extent	Little Extent	Great Extent	Completely

Have you any suggestions for improving the roleplays or for improving the procedure for using them?

What is your reaction to behavior modeling as a training approach?

Other comments or suggestions

Homework Assignment Sheet

Homework Assignment: Before the scheduled follow-up meeting, apply the learning points to at least one new on-the-job, performance-problem situation. (The *Learning Points Refresher Sheet* can serve as a handy reminder during the interview.)

Immediately after the interview, complete a *Learning Points Worksheet*. Record your reactions by each learning point you used, noting your experience with it and its effectiveness in the interaction.

What was the performance problem you dealt with? ______________________________

____

____

What was the person's apparent reaction to the interview ______________________________

____

Did the person carry out what s/he agreed to do?

____ No action to be taken ____ Too early to assess ____ No

____ Yes, very well ____ Yes, moderately well ____ Yes, very poorly

Any particular "lessons learned"? ______________________________

____

____

____

____

Note: This completed form, along with the accompanying *Learning Points Worksheet*, are for your records and to serve as reminders should you elect to report to the group.

YOU ARE NOT REQUIRED TO TURN ANYTHING IN

Homework Assignment Sheet

Homework Assignment: Before the scheduled follow-up meeting, apply the learning points to at least one new on-the-job, performance-problem situation. (The *Learning Points Refresher Sheet* can serve as a handy reminder during the interview.)

Immediately after the interview, complete a *Learning Points Worksheet*. Record your reactions by each learning point you used, noting your experience with it and its effectiveness in the interaction.

What was the performance problem you dealt with? ______________________________

____

____

What was the person's apparent reaction to the interview ______________________________

____

Did the person carry out what s/he agreed to do?

____ No action to be taken ____ Too early to assess ____ No

____ Yes, very well ____ Yes, moderately well ____ Yes, very poorly

Any particular "lessons learned"? ______________________________

____

____

____

____

Note: This completed form, along with the accompanying *Learning Points Worksheet*, are for your records and to serve as reminders should you elect to report to the group.

YOU ARE NOT REQUIRED TO TURN ANYTHING IN

Homework Assignment Sheet

Homework Assignment: Before the scheduled follow-up meeting, apply the learning points to at least one new on-the-job, performance-problem situation. (The *Learning Points Refresher Sheet* can serve as a handy reminder during the interview.)

Immediately after the interview, complete a *Learning Points Worksheet*. Record your reactions by each learning point you used, noting your experience with it and its effectiveness in the interaction.

What was the performance problem you dealt with? ________________________________

____

____

What was the person's apparent reaction to the interview ________________________________

____

Did the person carry out what s/he agreed to do?

____ No action to be taken ____ Too early to assess ____ No

____ Yes, very well ____ Yes, moderately well ____ Yes, very poorly

Any particular "lessons learned"? ________________________________

____

____

____

____

Note: This completed form, along with the accompanying *Learning Points Worksheet*, are for your records and to serve as reminders should you elect to report to the group.

YOU ARE NOT REQUIRED TO TURN ANYTHING IN

Homework Assignment Sheet

Homework Assignment: Before the scheduled follow-up meeting, apply the learning points to at least one new on-the-job, performance-problem situation. (The *Learning Points Refresher Sheet* can serve as a handy reminder during the interview.)

Immediately after the interview, complete a *Learning Points Worksheet*. Record your reactions by each learning point you used, noting your experience with it and its effectiveness in the interaction.

What was the performance problem you dealt with? ______________________________

____

____

What was the person's apparent reaction to the interview ______________________________

____

Did the person carry out what s/he agreed to do?

____ No action to be taken	____ Too early to assess	____ No
____ Yes, very well	____ Yes, moderately well	____ Yes, very poorly

Any particular "lessons learned"? ______________________________

____

____

____

____

Note: This completed form, along with the accompanying *Learning Points Worksheet*, are for your records and to serve as reminders should you elect to report to the group.

YOU ARE NOT REQUIRED TO TURN ANYTHING IN

Roleplay Input Form

Your Name ____

After getting acquainted with behavior modeling through the roleplays provided, it is important for you to practice applying the learning points to the types of real-life situations *you* are most likely to encounter. Think of a challenging individual, performance-problem situation that you have experienced, or observed, and *describe it below for those who will play the Supervisor and the Subordinate.*

Nature of subordinate's duties/responsibilities: ______________________________

____

____

Describe subordinate's work environment: ______________________________

____

____

Nature of the performance problem from the subordinate's viewpoint and knowledge at the time (if the subordinate was aware of a problem):

____

____

____

____

____

Describe the nature of the performance problem from the supervisor's viewpoint and knowledge at the time (regarding quality or quantity of work, tardiness, absenteeism, working with others, etc.):

____

____

____

Give any objective evidence the supervisor had to document the existence of the problem:

____

____

____

If the supervisor had previously talked to this subordinate about deficient performance, explain

____

____

____

Roleplay Input Form

Your Name ____

After getting acquainted with behavior modeling through the roleplays provided, it is important for you to practice applying the learning points to the types of real-life situations *you* are most likely to encounter. Think of a challenging individual, performance-problem situation that you have experienced, or observed, and *describe it below for those who will play the Supervisor and the Subordinate.*

Nature of subordinate's duties/responsibilities: ____

____

____

Describe subordinate's work environment: ____

____

____

Nature of the performance problem from the subordinate's viewpoint and knowledge at the time (if the subordinate was aware of a problem):

____

____

____

____

____

Describe the nature of the performance problem from the supervisor's viewpoint and knowledge at the time (regarding quality or quantity of work, tardiness, absenteeism, working with others, etc.):

____

____

____

Give any objective evidence the supervisor had to document the existence of the problem:

____

____

____

If the supervisor had previously talked to this subordinate about deficient performance, explain

____

____

____

Roleplay Input Form

Your Name ______________________________

After getting acquainted with behavior modeling through the roleplays provided, it is important for you to practice applying the learning points to the types of real-life situations *you* are most likely to encounter. Think of a challenging individual, performance-problem situation that you have experienced, or observed, and *describe it below for those who will play the Supervisor and the Subordinate.*

Nature of subordinate's duties/responsibilities: ______________________________

____

____

Describe subordinate's work environment: ______________________________

____

____

Nature of the performance problem from the subordinate's viewpoint and knowledge at the time (if the subordinate was aware of a problem):

____

____

____

____

____

Describe the nature of the performance problem from the supervisor's viewpoint and knowledge at the time (regarding quality or quantity of work, tardiness, absenteeism, working with others, etc.):

____

____

____

Give any objective evidence the supervisor had to document the existence of the problem:

____

____

____

If the supervisor had previously talked to this subordinate about deficient performance, explain

____

____

____

Roleplay Input Form

Your Name ____

After getting acquainted with behavior modeling through the roleplays provided, it is important for you to practice applying the learning points to the types of real-life situations *you* are most likely to encounter. Think of a challenging individual, performance-problem situation that you have experienced, or observed, and *describe it below for those who will play the Supervisor and the Subordinate.*

Nature of subordinate's duties/responsibilities: ________________________________

____

____

Describe subordinate's work environment: ________________________________

____

____

Nature of the performance problem from the subordinate's viewpoint and knowledge at the time (if the subordinate was aware of a problem):

____

____

____

____

____

Describe the nature of the performance problem from the supervisor's viewpoint and knowledge at the time (regarding quality or quantity of work, tardiness, absenteeism, working with others, etc.):

____

____

____

Give any objective evidence the supervisor had to document the existence of the problem:

____

____

____

If the supervisor had previously talked to this subordinate about deficient performance, explain

____

____

____

www.ingramcontent.com/pod-product-compliance
Ingram Content Group UK Ltd.
Pitfield, Milton Keynes, MK11 3LW, UK
UKHW051507290926
15471UKWH00008B/1483

9 781607 520955